AUTOMOBILES

BY
DAVID CORBETT

The Horseless Carriage

OLD POWER, NEW TYRES

One interesting achievement was that of R.W. Thompson who built the first vehicle to run on rubber tyres. They were fitted to horse-drawn carriages. Thompson also patented the first pneumatic tyre: this had a leather outer cover with several tubes inside. This invention was unknown to William Dunlop when he 're-invented' the pneumatic tyre for bicycles in 1888.

No event has changed our lives so much as the invention of the motor car. Love it or hate it, the motor car is the most successful form of transport, and for most people it has become an essential part of daily life. In common with most inventions, there is a story stretching back into history which charts the development of the motor car. Records exist of plans for a sail-driven vehicle. This was the dream of Guido da Vigevano in 1335, but there is no evidence of the vehicle ever being made. By the late 18th century, steam seemed to be an obvious source of power for the horseless carriage, and some weird and wonderful steam-driven vehicles appeared. Englishman Richard Trevithick had always been interested in steam and, in 1803, he invented a steam road-coach, which could carry eight passengers at 19 km/h (12 mph). He lost interest after one eventful night, when he left his coach in a shed next to an inn without damping down the fire. Coach and shed were both destroyed – just one reason why inventors started to look for alternative power.

AHEAD OF HIS TIME

Leonardo da Vinci, who was born in 1452, had a brilliant mind. His designs foretold many of our existing forms of transport – the submarine, the helicopter, and even a horseless carriage. There is no proof that this vehicle was ever made, but a clockwork model does exist. It was a tricycle with tiller steering on the front single wheel and a differential gear on the rear wheels. This allowed the outside wheel on a corner to turn faster than the inside wheel. It was, in itself, a remarkable invention.

THINGS THAT GO BUMP IN THE NIGHT

This early 19th-century cartoon depicts a rather fanciful design for a steam-driven vehicle. In Cornwall, a man named William Murdoch made a similar machine, using a small model steam engine attached to a child's tricycle. Whilst trying it out one night, it ran away from him and was said to have terrorized the local vicar!

THE START OF IT ALL

The credit for the first vehicle to move under its own power has to be given to the Frenchman Nicholas Cugnot in 1769. It was a steam-powered tricycle with a huge boiler in front of the single front wheel (left). Because of the weight on this single wheel, steering was very difficult. It was recorded that, on its first outing, it knocked down a wall. A reconstruction of this machine can be seen at the *Conservatoire des Arts et Métiers* in Paris. With a top speed of 3 km/h (2 mph), it was never a success and there was no immediate development.

THE FIRST CAR IN AMERICA

The first recorded horseless carriage in the United States is thought to be an amphibious dredge called *Orukter Amphibolos,* built by Oliver Evans.

THE STEAM COACH

Like other operators, this James' Steam Coach of 1829 began coach services carrying passengers. Disaster struck on 29 July 1834. A wheel on John Scott Russell's steam coach collapsed, the boiler exploded and five passengers were killed. This was just what the opponents of road vehicles wanted. Most had interests in the up-and-coming railways and they managed to get road tolls increased and laws passed which severely restricted the development of motor vehicles for many years.

EMILE LEVASSOR

In the Paris Exhibition of 1889, Emile Levassor saw a Daimler car for the first time. He thought the car itself was poor but was intrigued by its engine. Daimler had given a licence to build the engine to his attorney who died, the licence then becoming the property of the attorney's attractive widow. Levassor, who had been a friend of her husband, fell in love with her and they married. Under French law the licence became his. Levassor built his first car with the engine placed in the middle under the passenger seat but later placed it in front. This became the first of what was to become the traditional layout of car design.

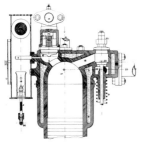

THE 'HOT TUBE' IGNITION ENGINE

Engines were comparatively simple at this time, but the water jacket to cool down the engine came in very quickly. Valves to allow the petrol/air mixture into the cylinder and the exhaust gases to escape were very simple. An internal explosion was caused by the tube (on the left of the diagram) being heated up by a petrol flame. This went through the cylinder wall where it ignited the fuel. The timing was somewhat haphazard, and an explosion sometimes took place when the exhaust valve was open – hence the title of the film – 'Chitty, Chitty, BANG! BANG!'

1898 CANNSTATT DAIMLER

It has been said that Daimler was an old fuddy-duddy to have produced such an old-fashioned car so late in his life. The Cannstatt was like a horse-drawn Brougham carriage with the horses taken away. The basic design of the car worked well: it was simple to drive and the 4-horsepower engine meant that the maximum speed was about 26 km/h (16 mph). After Daimler's death, the Cannstatt was developed into the first Mercedes

The Dawn of Motoring

The first cars driven by an internal combustion engine did not use petrol as a fuel, but a mixture of coal, gas and air. In 1860, a Frenchman called Lenoir designed the first gas engine. The gas was introduced into a large cylinder where a spark caused an explosion which drove a piston. An Austrian, Siegfried Markus, worked on engines powered by petrol. He mounted one in a hand-cart in 1864, and this has a claim to be the first petrol-driven car ever made. He lost interest however, and it was left to others to make and sell the new motor carriages. Although many people had a hand in the development of the motor car, two Germans stand out as having had a major input; Gottlieb Daimler and Karl Benz. Although these men worked separately, they were the first to construct and sell motor cars to the public.

1884 BENZ

Karl Benz came from a poor family but began to make a success of his life when he produced his first motor tricycle. The top speed was about 13 km/h (8 mph). It is said that his wife took her two sons to see her mother in the tricycle, a distance of some 100 km (62 miles), but had to stop at the chemist shop in order to buy petrol. In those days petrol was an unwanted by-product from the production of lamp oil and was sold in a chemist shop for medicinal reasons. Later, when the car broke down, she is said to have repaired it using elastic from her garter.

DAIMLER AND MAYBACH

Gottlieb Daimler made gas engines for the firm of Otto and Langan. With his friend, Wilhelm Maybach, he produced the 'Otto Silent Gas Engine', which is accepted as the world's first four-stroke engine. He left the firm when he was 48 and, along with Maybach, moved to Cannstatt. Here, they produced a small light engine which ran on liquid fuel. He bought a second-hand carriage, removed the shafts and installed one of his engines.

ONE OF THE FIRST POSTERS

Karl Benz took his car to the Paris Exhibition in 1887 and began to attract sales. He used an agent, Emile Roger, to sell his cars in France and so the motor car industry was started. In order to attract custom, advertising was used, a feature which has carried on to this day.

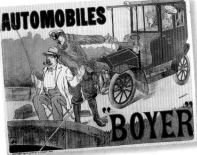

Early Automobiles

The development of early automobiles was most pronounced in countries closest to their birthplace in Germany. Just as happens today, development was a result of racing. The first races took place on ordinary roads and between large towns. Firms such as De Dion-Bouton, who were based just outside Paris, gained popularity through winning races, which were avidly followed by the press of the day. Firms in Great Britain suffered because of the restrictive laws, which set the top speed of a car at 6 km/h (4 mph) in the country and 3 km/h (2 mph) in town. Early cars had no uniformity in design; without the horses, the carriage was now steered in a variety of ways. Some firms used the wheel, others copied the tiller of a boat or the handlebars of a bicycle. The bodywork copied the carriage, using the skills of the existing workforce. Much of it was in wood with leather seats. Cars at this time are best described as 'the playthings of the rich'.

I'M TRYING TO GET PAST

The relationship between the motorist and the rest of the population was, to say the least, strained. Cars were said to ruin the crops with the dust they produced as they went along the road, their exhaust was poisonous and they would kill people and animals when they went out of control. Much of the protest was orchestrated by interested parties, such as horse breeders and shareholders in the railways, who saw the possibility of their income being reduced.

DRIVING BY CANDLELIGHT

The first lamps were lit by a candle; they usually had a long tube underneath which contained a spring to push up the candle as it burnt down. They gave very little light and so oil lamps were later used, as on this 1903 De Dion (right).

BEEP!

In order to warn people of their approach, motorists used various devices. The most common was the horn, like this one, which was a bugle with a rubber bulb!

THE STARTING HANDLE

To start the car, the motorist had to turn a starting handle. Even with a small engine this was very difficult and dangerous to turn. Many arms were broken as a result of poor technique. It was also the reason why ladies seldom drove cars at this time.

THE ENGINE

Many of the early cars had small engines. This De Dion engine is typical. There was no petrol pump and so the petrol was fed from the tank by gravity. This worked well for the most part but, when going up a steep hill, the tank dropped below the level of the engine and so the petrol ceased to flow. To continue, the car had to be turned round and reversed up the hill.

GEAR CHANGE

There were many ways of changing gear. In this case the De Dion had a lever on the left of the steering column – pull backward for first gear and away for second gear. The reverse gear was engaged by pressing down a pedal with the right heel. The advance/retard lever and the accelerator lever are both seen on the right of the steering column.

1903 DE DION

This is a typical example of an early Edwardian car. There was little or no protection for the motorist and so most of the motoring would have taken place during the summer. The wheels were made of wood and the tyres were pneumatic, replacing the solid rubber tyre of the late Victorian period. This would mean frequent stops to repair punctures, mainly caused by horseshoe nails on the road.

ELEGANT HEADWARE

Motoring clothing for both sexes was advertised in catalogues. Ladies' hats needed to be securely fastened with a scarf or several hat pins, and veils in front kept out the dust that rose in clouds from the dry summer roads. In winter, gentlemen had heavy coats, some with a detachable leather lining to keep out the cold. Ladies would have a large foot warmer filled with hot water.

EARLY WINDSCREENS

In order to wear more fashionable hats in an open top car, folding windscreens were often used. Many were built into the front of the back seat and could be unfolded quickly when required.

Status & Comfort

With the advent of larger cars, motorists demanded more luxury. They employed chauffeurs to drive their cars, although the chauffeurs no longer had to light a fire to build up steam, as their name suggests (chauffer means 'to heat up' in French). They wore uniforms which signified their employer's status. The car had become a status symbol. Cars were exported to countries such as India, where the local maharajah would drive in a most exotic car displaying a level of luxury befitting his station in life. Royal patronage was a distinct advantage. The Daimler company derived great benefit from having the Prince of Wales, later to become King Edward VII of England, as a patron. Protection from the weather became more important as the use of the car gradually changed from a rich person's plaything to a useful part of everyday life. Open cars gave way to cars with hoods and then to enclosed passenger areas.

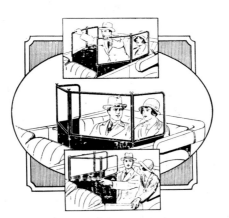

MOTORING CLOTHES

The motorists seen here are wearing clothes typical of 1909. The car does have a windscreen but, due to the lack of windscreen wipers, it had to be moved when it rained in order to see the road. There is also a basket for a parasol, in case the sun should come out.

OUT FOR THE DAY

'A beautiful day for a picnic, if it should rain we can always retire to the enclosed back of the car. It means that we can wear more elegant clothing as befits our station in life. The chauffeur does have a windscreen but when we drive in the rain that has to be fastened up into the roof.'

THE ULTIMATE IN LUXURY

The inside of the passenger compartment could be built to the owner's specification. Many were designed as copies of first class railway carriages with windows that opened and adjusted by way of a leather belt. Some had speaking tubes, so that the chauffeur could be given instructions whilst on the move. Inside would be opulent, velvet upholstery, with blinds on each window. Quite often the top of the car would have a protective railing to hold personal luggage when the family went on holiday. The bulk of the luggage and the servants would precede the family to make certain everything was ready for them when they arrived.

At the Garage

Until the turn of the century, the commercial garage didn't exist. Repairs to the car were carried out by the owner or his chauffeur. Punctures had to be repaired on the road and, because wheels couldn't be removed from the car, they were repaired as we mend bicycle tyres today, by removing the inner tube and repairing the hole. The first garages evolved, some from workshops for agricultural repairs and others from bicycle repair shops. Most were in county towns or large market towns for the simple reason that this is where the gentry or professional men, such as doctors, could be found. The first petrol pumps were seen about 1910. Petrol was raised from an underground tank, by means of a hand pump, into a glass tank where the customer could see it, and then released into the petrol tank of the car. Each garage sold different makes of petrol and, on the road leading up to the garage, a miscellany of advertising boards extolled the virtues of their petrol.

OIL CAN

When early motorists bought oil from a garage, it was pumped from a big oil drum into a small can, usually carrying the advertising slogan of the oil company. There were different size cans for the amount of oil you needed. The oil was then poured into your car.

PUNCTURE REPAIRS

Punctures were very frequent even as late as 1908 when this picture was taken. In order to make a good repair a 'vulcanizer' was used. This consisted of a metal tank which fastened around the inner tyre holding the patch against the hole in the inner tyre. Methylated spirits was poured into the tank and lit. The resulting fire was just hot enough to weld the rubber patch to the tyre, so creating a strong bond.

SPARKING PLUGS

The insulation on older spark plugs often broke down and the wise motorist always carried spares. These were often stored in tin boxes or wooden cylinders. The oil system of early cars was primitive and so oily plugs often had to be cleaned when on a journey. Deposits on the electrodes had to be brushed off frequently.

AMERICAN GARAGE

Garages around the world evolved in much the same way as in Europe. Bicycle and machine repair shops became garages offering the motorist a number of services. Most supplied air for the tyres because they lost air relatively quickly; some even sold their air, so much per tyre. Water was available to top up the radiator when required. Suppliers names were prominent both on the building and in the road approaching the garage.

GARAGE INTERIOR

Many early cars had to be serviced every 800 km (500 miles) and so early garages were busy places. Many, in addition to dealing with cars, repaired bicycles, charged accumulators for radios and sold chocolate and cigarettes. The mechanics had to have a knowledge of a variety of makes of car and be able to manufacture parts whenever possible.

PETROL CANS

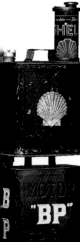

Before the advent of the petrol pump, petrol was sold in nine-litre (two-gallon) cans. The cap was made of brass as careless use with an iron cap might cause a spark which could lead to an explosion. The cap had turrets on top so that a lever could be used to open them. A lead seal guaranteed that no petrol could be removed after leaving the refinery. Each can would bear the firm's name.

ATTRACTING THE CUSTOMERS

Advertising your services became important as more garages appeared and some of it took on an art form of its own.

OLDSMOBILE

Ransom E. Olds started making steam-driven and petrol-driven cars with his father in 1890. His 1902 curved dashboard runabout (left) became the first car to be made in real quantity production. He had a machine shop down which the cars passed, having one operation completed at each bench. His backers wanted to build large cars and so he sold out. The company was bought by William Durant, who also bought the firm of a Scotsman called David Dunbar Buick, keeping the name. In 1908, Durant created General Motors by adding the firms of Cadillac and Oakland to Buick and Oldsmobile.

MERCEDES

Emile Jellinek, the Austro-Hungarian consul in Nice, was the agent for Daimler cars. He persuaded Maybach, Daimler's partner, and Paul, Daimler's son, to produce a brand new car with many new features. The sides were made of pressed metal instead of wood, the radiator needed half the water and it used internal expanding brakes. The car (a 1903 model shown right) was named after the agent's daughter, Mercedes. Another Austro-Daimler car was named after a second daughter Maja but this was later dropped in favour of the name of the technical director – Ferdinand Porsche.

FIAT

Italy started her motor industry later than the other European countries. There were several small firms, none of whom made any great impression until a group of men got together to form the Fabbrica Italiana Automobili Torino, or Fiat for short. They built a small four-seater car where the passengers sat opposite the driver. The firm quickly took off and started exporting to America. This Fiat ran in the 1912 French Grand Prix.

Early Firms

RENAULT

I t has been said that with the early motor cars it was a battle to make them go at all. By 1907, however, the motor car became fairly reliable. Daimler's patents on his engines were sold and became the bedrock on which the motor industries of Great Britain and Austria were built. Count Albert De Dion and his partner, Georges Bouton, produced magnificent small engines, light and powerful. They were used by many other firms: Darracq, Delage, Peugeot and Renault in France; Humber in Britain; Adler in Germany; Ceirano in Italy; and Peerless and Pierce Arrow in America. Having made their start, these firms then went on to produce their own engines and become, if only for a time, giants in the motoring world. As time passed many of the early firms were amalgamated or went bankrupt. Many of the famous names are now only to be found in the museums of the world.

Louis Renault was hopeless at school but started to teach himself about engines in his garden shed in France. Like others, he bought a De Dion tricycle but converted it to a four wheeler. He then made a car of his own, using a De Dion engine. Renault was the first person to use a propeller shaft to drive the wheels, rather than chains. His cars quickly became popular and so, helped by his two brothers, the firm of Renault was started. This picture shows a 1906 Renault with its rear compartment based on a first class railway carriage.

ROLLS ROYCE

One of the most famous partnerships began in 1904 between Charles Rolls (right) and Henry Royce (left). The two came from very different backgrounds. Rolls was well educated and from a wealthy home; Royce was poor and had to start work at the age of 12. After finishing an engineering apprenticeship, he started a small firm making electric cranes and dynamos in Manchester. Having driven a French Decauville he thought he could do much better and so, in 1903, he built his first car. Rolls also knew a lot about cars, being a racing driver. He sold cars in Mayfair, a famous part of London, and was looking for a good English car for his showroom. Rolls liked Royce's car and agreed to sell as many as he could produce. In 1906 they produced the Silver Ghost, so called because of its silent running. It was admired for its reliability and refinement and stayed in production for 19 years. The Rolls Royce Motor Company had started.

Mass Production

When cars were first produced, it was on the basis of a potential owner ordering his car and only then was the car built. In the workshop, cars were built individually by a number of workers, each with a different skill. This was a costly way to build a car and so motor cars were very much confined to rich people.

Ransom Olds is thought to be the first person to start an assembly line to produce his cars. It was made easier by the fact that his workshop burnt down. He needed to produce cars quickly and so hit upon this idea of moving the car down a line. Although he didn't know it at the time, this was the start of a revolution within the motor car industry, which would drastically reduce the price of a car and so put it within the range of the ordinary working man.

THE MASTER OF MASS PRODUCTION

From his boyhood days Henry Ford was said to be a master of mechanical logic. He always dreamed of making a car and, as he was a demonstrator of steam engines, he initially thought in terms of steam. It was when he read about internal combustion engines in magazines sent from England that he knew where the future lay. When Ford visited an exhibition in Chicago and saw a display of Daimler engines, he returned home and made his own engine out of scrap materials. This was the start of the Ford dream.

1908 – MODEL T PRODUCTION LINE

Although not the first, Ford's production line was the best, mainly due to Ford's detailed research. Every aspect was timed, and detailed planning made certain that progress was quick and that no time was wasted. The car's body was manufactured on the upper floor and then lowered on to the chassis, which had been manufactured on the lower floor. Ford more than doubled the wages of his workers, and the cost per car fell, until even the workers could afford to buy their own. By 1928, 15 million Model Ts had been produced.

THE TIN LIZZIE

Perhaps Ford's most successful car was the Model T. It had a variety of forms. As well as being a car it could be a bus or a tractor. The blossoming film industry of the time was quick to see the potential of the motor car and many Model Ts were featured. The famous expression 'You can have it in any colour as long as it's black' was because the black paint dried quicker than any other colour and so speeded up the production line.

TODAY'S ROBOT ARMY

The car factory of today is a far different place. Computers are everywhere. Robotic arms swoop in as a car passes to spot-weld the panels together. In the paint room, robotic spray guns, controlled by a computer, paint the car in such a way that the minimum amount of paint is used.

THE 1950s – MIND YOUR HEAD

Mass production in the 1950s was still very labour intensive and the cost per unit high. Cars in this Renault plant moved around the factory floor using aerial railways. Renault went through a difficult period after the Second World War; the firm was nationalized by Charles de Gaulle and there was a lot of political and union unrest.

THE 1920s – IT MAY TAKE TIME, BUT WE GET THERE!

The Humber Motorcar Company started, like many others, by making bicycles. The firm later made aeroplane engines but were always renowned for their excellently built cars. Although using a form of mass production, Humber put quality first and so cost per unit was relatively high.

The 1920s

*T*he 1920s are sometimes called 'The Golden Age of Motoring'. It was a time of great change both socially and within the motor car industry. There was little traffic on the road and few legal restrictions. Women experienced a new-found freedom in driving. Some had driven ambulances and other vehicles during the Great War and, with the introduction of the electric self-starter and improved gear boxes, were just as capable of driving as men. Although mass production was causing a fall in price, motoring was still for the rich and the professional.

This was the time of the luxury car and the emergence of the sports car, featuring large engines and a top speed approaching 160 km/h (100 mph). Many of them used engines that were developed for aeroplanes during the War. The aeroplane industry was also the source of inspiration for the first attempts to streamline cars. In order to test these new high-speed cars, Fiat built a banked track on top of their factory; later used in the film *The Italian Job*.

A CAR FOR THE STARS

Between the wars, Isotta-Fraschini was the leading maker of luxury cars in Italy. Their cars never quite matched those of Rolls Royce or Hispano-Suiza, but were popular in America amongst celebrities.

THE KING'S CAR

The Hispano-Suiza Tulip Wood H6 was of Spanish/ French origin and was a car whose engineering qualities were world famous. The patronage by King Alfonso XIII of Spain meant that these cars were aimed at the rich and were the continental rivals of Rolls Royce cars.

COUNTRY ROADS

As a result of there being very few cars on the road, motoring was a pleasurable experience. Trips into the countryside were popular. Many of the roads were not really built for the motor car, but that only added to the excitement. Picnics in the open were the order of the day.

A VERY FAST CAR

The son of an Italian artist, Ettore Bugatti was apprenticed to a Milan machine shop. When he moved to Alsace in 1907, he soon started to make his own cars, like this Type 43 built in 1927. His cars became very successful on the race track and won many races. The radiator front of his cars is said to be in the shape of a horse shoe because Bugatti loved horses and had stables at his factory.

WOMEN DRIVERS

A sight rarely seen before, a lady driving a car. The motoring press was full of letters from irate men saying that women should stay at home but, for women, it meant freedom and, from this time on, they took full advantage of their new position within society.

ROOM FOR ONE MORE, SIR!

Trips to certain tourist centres could result in chaos when it came to parking your car. The seaside was especially popular and local land owners realized that they could make money by charging people to park on their land. This American beach, photographed in 1924, lured many motorists, showing that the motor trade was really taking off in the USA. Car racing on the beach became popular in Daytona, with farmers selling produce beside the road.

The 1930s

These were the years of the Great Depression. Many car firms were lost or taken over by larger groups. At the same time there was a race to produce the first car under £100 in Great Britain, one that was affordable for a lot of families. A similar race was taking place in Germany to produce a 'Car for the People', or 'Volks Wagen' in German. Great advances were made in electrical equipment, suspension and tyres during this time. Synchronized gears made gear changing easier, but cars had to have oil heaters placed under them in cold weather as antifreeze was not generally available. There were no such things as car heaters and every few thousand kilometres your car had to be taken to a garage to have the valves ground – decarbonization. Citroën produced the revolutionary front-wheel drive but, in doing so, Andre Citroën extended his factory so much that he had money troubles and lost control of the firm.

AN EVENING OUT

Posters continued to show prestigious cars in most glamorous situations. In this Fiat poster of 1938, you can see very stylish ladies arriving for an evening out. Advertisers hoped to create the impression that, in order to be seen as successful people, you had to have one of their cars.

A LOT OF CAR

Emile Delahaye took over the Delage Motor Company in 1935 and produced cars which were both beautiful to behold and which performed well. Delahaye was also noted for making fast motorboats and supplying taxi cabs to New York. The styling was streamlined but curvaceous and was the forerunner of things to come.

PUNCTURE PROBLEMS

Due to the improvement in tyre technology and the better road surfaces, there were fewer punctures. When one did occur, replacing a wheel was much easier with the introduction of devices such as the in-built jack.

IN A CLASS BY ITSELF

THE BEST
YOU CAN BUY

Fred and August, the two
Duesenburg brothers, moved
to America from Germany in
1884. They both loved cars and
Fred became a famous racing driver.
They produced successful racing cars and
later branched out into passenger cars like
this 1933 model. Their cars were, as you might
imagine, very fast. They had several new features, including indicators to let
you know when the engine oil needed changing and when the battery needed
topping up. Several coach builders on both sides of the Atlantic built some of
the most beautiful bodies for the cars.

LOOKS GOOD, BUT...

It is said that the beautiful body of the Auburn concealed indifferent engineering. Errett Cord took over the firm
when it was in difficulty and built supercharged cars capable of going at 160 km/h (100 mph). Some had a built-in
radio and a special compartment for golf clubs.

Für sportliches Fahren
auf Sonderwunsch mit Sporttüren aus Leichtmetall und Sportscheibe

Zur weiteren Gewichtsverminderung können die Stoßstangen und auch das Verdeck abgeschraubt werden

The 1940s & 1950s

During the Second World War domestic car production all over the world came to a standstill. Everything was geared to the war effort. When the War was over, manufacturers

IN A CLASS OF ITS OWN

Mercedes made a name for itself with cars of excellent quality, strength, durability, performance and roadholding. Their success in racing, due to sophisticated engineering, left other famous makes lagging behind them and boosted their sales.

A horrific crash at Le Mans in 1955 involving a Mercedes 300 SLR resulted in Daimler-Benz withdrawing from motor racing.

continued to make the type of car that had been sold earlier. At the end of the 1940s, however, new designs started to appear on the market. The American designs displayed an abundance of chrome, and the bulbous bodies had fins on the back, which seemed to increase in size as time went by. Front bench seats and gear sticks on the steering column both became popular features. Running boards and separate mudguards were phasing out. The Volkswagen Beetle was first produced at this time to become the most popular car in the world (see page 28), and other firms started to produce small economical cars. Firms who didn't change with the times went bankrupt and many famous names disappeared.

A VERY POPULAR CAR.

Although very basic, the British-made Ford Popular was a very successful car. The fittings were minimal, which made it 20 per cent cheaper than the opposition, but with a performance better than some larger-engined cars.

NVX 370

MESSENGER OF THE GODS

Several British and American firms used Mercury as their trade name but it was the Ford Motor Company that made it famous. They used Ford engines but a different body – it was the start of 'badge engineering' – almost identical cars being sold under different names. The cars were longer, lower and wider but have been said to be some of the ugliest cars made.

STRAIGHT OUT OF TOMORROW
1957 Mercury

WITH *DREAM-CAR DESIGN*

SPECTACULAR MOTORING

Antoine de la Mothe Cadillac was the French officer who founded the city of Detroit as a fur trading centre in 1701. The family had a coat of arms dating from the 11th century and this remains the only authentic coat of arms to be used on an American car to this day. William Murphy chose this name for his car-making firm and employed one Henry Ford to design his cars. Ford had a disagreement with the firm's backers and left, but the company went on to prosper. The Eldorado (left) was typical of the American cars of the period: big-engined with lots of chrome.

THE SOLDIER'S WORKHORSE

The Jeep was first built in response to a U.S. Government competition. It asked makers to design a car which could operate in difficult situations, be sturdy and reliable, but easily repaired if it did break down. Willys were given the contract but Ford also made the vehicle. In fact the name Jeep came from the Ford designation 'G.P.', meaning General Purpose.

OLD-FASHIONED BUT SOLID

In the War, Field Marshal Montgomery used a Humber car typical of the early 1940s. Big and solid, it was the type of car used by senior officers all over the world. Makes varied according to the country, but the style was the same. Many of the cars were armour plated making them very heavy, but they were powered by large engines.

FIRE! FIRE!

The first fire engines were horse drawn and run by insurance companies. They would only put out a fire in houses insured by that company. Later models like this French Gobron Brillie Engine of 1907 had a petrol engine, but relied on a steam pump to provide the power for the water jets.

ALL ABOARD THE 1928 BUS

Because of the great distances between towns, countries such as America had an extensive bus service. In some ways they copied the old stage coaches where journeys were so long they had to be completed in several stages over many days. Some early coaches used existing cars such as the Model T Ford and extended the chassis to take more passengers.

WHAT'S THE WEATHER LIKE UP THERE?

This Parisian cab is by no means unusual and probably has its origins in the Hansom Cab, a horse-drawn cab with the driver in a similar position. There was usually a trap door in the roof with which to communicate with the passenger.

THE LONDON CAB

One of the best loved features of the streets of London is the London taxi. When the car started to take over from horse-drawn vehicles, some were used to transport people around town. There were rest huts erected where the 'cabbie' could put his feet up and have a cup of tea. Almost all of these have now disappeared.

Commercial Vehicles

Commercial vehicles went through great change in the 1930s. Before that time horse-drawn carts delivered the milk and coal, and steam-driven lorries were used to deliver heavy goods. Now mass-produced light vans and diesel vans took over. Charabancs and coaches were used for excursions and 'mystery trips' into the surrounding countryside. Some vehicles, in addition to their use as delivery vans, were used for advertising; in some cases it was confined to a picture and slogan on the side of the van, in others it was more elaborate. Today, commercial vehicles deliver just about everything we buy in shops. We have vehicles to deliver petrol, ready-mixed concrete, furniture and even nuclear fuel. Container lorries now also make the transfer of goods to merchant ships a very easy job.

YOU CAN'T SQUEEZE ME!

Some vehicles were used exclusively for advertising. This Orange advertised a brand of South African oranges. It was, in fact, a mini car with a fibre glass top. All the windows except the windscreen were orange, so giving a warm glow inside. It was dangerous to exceed 48 km/h (30 mph) as a touch of the brakes at this speed might start the orange rolling!

1907   *1950*   *1997*   *1999*

1907 Some taxis had open storage compartments beside the driver where luggage could be strapped up. They also had 'For Hire' arms which told you if the taxi was available for hire. This had a meter which showed the fare due as you went along. *1950* Taxis later became enclosed with the meter on the inside. *1997* Although similar in shape, the taxis now had air conditioning, pull-down child seats and facilities for passengers with wheelchairs. *1999* The traditional black cab is slowly being replaced by cabs of all colours; some are now moving advertisements.

Motor Racing

MIND THE CAR!

The last major race to be held entirely on ordinary roads is the Monaco Grand Prix. This photograph was taken during the 1933 race, which was a hard-fought race between top Italian rivals Achille Varzi and Tazio Nuvolari (with Varzi the eventual winner). Today's spectators are kept well out of the way of the road, but in these early days many people were killed after failing to get out of the way in time.

*T*he first motor races were held on public roads in France. They were usually between two towns and were governed by strict rules. The first race was between Paris and Rouen in 1894, when there were 102 contestants. It is disputed how many cars actually started, as most were disqualified for one reason or another. One driver allowed to stay in the race promptly drove into his brother's car, then into a cafe, and finally into a ditch before he retired. Remarkably, most of the others finished. The following year, the race was from Paris to Bordeaux and back again. Emile Levassor won, having driven for 48 hours with no relief driver. He was disqualified for having only two seats in his car – the rules stated there should be four – but the publicity was good for him and he sold lots of cars. The first Grand Prix was in 1906 on a 103-km (64-mile) circuit near Le Mans. The cars by this time were monsters with an engine capacity of up to 20 litres (4 gallons).

MODERN-DAY HEROES

The racing driver of today has worked his way up from junior racing and can command very high wages. The car he drives is as safe as can be made, being able to survive high-speed crashes. Even the clothing is designed to protect him in the event of a serious fire. Nevertheless it is a dangerous profession and many well-known figures have been killed or forced to retire through serious injury.

HANG ON TIGHT!

Other countries were quick to organize races, some of which are still remembered to this day. This one shows the Targa Florio rally in Italy and shows the mechanic sitting in the side seat hanging on for dear life. William K. Vanderbilt promoted racing in America and was the first American to hold the world land speed record. He organized the first race at Long Island using public roads and, at one point, the drivers had to cross a railway line.

THE WORLD'S RICHEST RACE

This 'Indy' car is specially designed for the Indianapolis 500 – a name that conjures up images of spectacularly fast racing. In 1908, Carl G. Fisher decided that the motor industry in America needed a racing and test track. He bought a farm for $72,000 and built a track that had two long straights with four banked corners. This enabled the cars to go faster. The success of the track was established in 1911, when the prize money of $25,000 attracted a good field and 80,000 spectators. From that time the annual race has gone from strength to strength, becoming the richest race in the world.

MADE IT!

This is M. Vachheron who came fourth in the Paris to Rouen race of 1894. The first across the line was Albert de Dion, but he was disqualified as it was said that he wasn't driving a car but a steam tractor pulling a passenger coach. His average speed was 18 km/h (11 mph). In 1903, a race was held on a figure-of-eight course in Ireland. One driver had difficulty in starting – the starter kept calling, 'Go! Go!' until it was pointed out that the driver was French. One 'Allez!' and the driver was off – as far as the first corner where he rolled down a bank into the river.

RACING COLOURS

The colour of racing cars was picked to show the country of its origin. This Lotus bore the racing green colour of England. Now Grand Prix cars are covered in advertising which helps pay for the upkeep of the racing team.

Design: Successes & Failures

GO ANYWHERE, DO ANYTHING

In its various forms the Landrover can be found all over the world. Not beautiful to look at, even in its upmarket forms, but very practical. Its four-wheel drive and low gearing enable it to go where other transport dares not go. The aluminium body panels do not rust and can be easily replaced if damaged. It is used for a variety of purposes – fire engines, safari transport, farming, to name a few.

When the idea of a horseless carriage first entered peoples' minds, that is just what it was – a carriage without horses. Gradually people began to think of motor cars as something different and they looked for alternative designs. Certain things could not change: there had to be wheels; a chassis strong enough to support the engine; somewhere for the driver and passengers to sit, and so on. Ideas were copied from existing forms of transport. Gradually, motor cars were made to look attractive as people's tastes were considered. Motor car design has also been affected by changes in technology. Modern engine design enables us to do things that were not possible in the past. The different functions now required of a motor car also determine, to a certain extent, its styling. Sports cars need low weight concentration, and widely spaced wheels; Presidential cars need bomb-proof bodies and bullet-proof glass; family saloons need space for passengers and for weekly shopping trips. The list is endless.

THE CAR OF ITS GENERATION

If ever a car represented its time in Britain, it must be the Mini. Now much copied, it was brilliantly designed by Alec Issigonis. The Swinging 60s, with its many social changes, needed a car that was different and reflected the mood of the country – they certainly had it with the Mini. A small car but with lots of space for the passengers, and a small engine compartment with the engine turned sideways to take up less room.

THE CAR FOR THE RICH YOUNG MAN

Porsche was probably one of the finest designers of the motor car. It was often said that he was an artist, but it was also said that he couldn't draw a straight line. He had the ability to communicate to his draughtsmen in such a way that they could put down on paper exactly what he was thinking. His designs broke new ground and other car makers were in awe of the cars he produced. Many of his original ideas have been copied by other car manufacturers.

THE BUBBLE CAR

The Bubble car, of which the BMW Isetta is a good example, was very popular and very adventurous in design. Entry was by a front door which opened outward. On many models there was no reverse gear, which could cause problems if you parked up against a wall – how to get out! Some models had only three wheels.

MASCOTS

The first mascot on a vehicle is thought to have been found on a chariot buried with Tutankhamun; it was a sun-crested falcon put there to bring good luck.

The Jaguar was first seen on the Swallow Company's SS Jaguar of 1936. Gordon Crosby designed it and it was used until 1960 when, after being reduced in size, it was withdrawn when safety laws were introduced.

Hispano-Suiza cars were Spanish but built in Spain and France. They used a flying stork in honour of George Guynemer, a popular flying ace of the First World War. It was the emblem of his squadron.

The Spirit of Ecstasy is perhaps the best-known emblem. It was made for Rolls Royce by Charles Sykes, an eminent artist and sculptor, at the suggestion of the second Lord Montagu. Sykes is said to have used Lord Montagu's secretary as a model.

THERE FOR ALL TO SEE

There is always a great conflict with designing cars for famous people. They need to be on open view where everyone can see them, yet they need to be protected from those who would do them harm. The Pope-mobile, as it came to be called, was a Range Rover adaptation which had a 'viewing room' at the back. This proved to be popular both with the public, who had a good view, but also with the Pope who was protected not only from those who might harm him, but also from the weather.

The Immortals

Every now and again a car comes along that grabs the public imagination. It may do so for a variety of reasons – its design, its engineering, even its notoriety. These are the cars people want to own or to see. When cars appear in motion pictures they create an impression, especially when the car does something out of the ordinary: *Herbie,* the VW Beetle with a mind of its own; the DeLorean which takes you *Back to the Future; Genevieve,* the old car which refused to give up and, in doing so, created worldwide interest in Veteran and Vintage cars. Some cars are admired as works of art, and it has been known for some people to have particularly beautiful cars in their homes, as a form of three-dimensional art.

THE MOST POPULAR CAR IN THE WORLD

Designed by Porsche, the Volkswagen Beetle was rejected by the British car industry as being too ugly. It went on to sell more cars than any other, outselling the previous record holder, the Model T Ford. It was popular with all ages, and, having an air-cooled engine, there was no need for anti-freeze in the winter.

A FARMER'S CAR

Pierre Boulanger was asked by Citroen to produce a car which could carry, in addition to the farmer's wife and a pig in the back, a basket of eggs that would not break even when driving across a ploughed field. The result was the Citroen 2CV, which has been compared to an umbrella with four wheels underneath. Andre Citroen started life as a maker of gears and his most successful had teeth shaped like a chevron – this became the sign he put on the front of his cars, and which can be seen to this day.

A CAR FULL OF GADGETS

The films featuring James Bond have always used spectacular gadgets and this car is no exception. It started life as an Aston Martin DB5, but was transformed by the addition of revolving number plates, machine guns in the front, oil spray at the back, back bullet-proof plate and, best of all, an ejecting passenger seat which could send your passenger through the roof.

A STATUS SYMBOL

The E-Type Jaguar was the cult car of the 1960s. It was a road car with the performance of a racing car. Beautiful to look at, but with very simple lines, it was admired by all. Its top speed of 241 km/h (150 mph) made it popular, as did its price, which was considerably less than other comparable makes. Its one big fault was its petrol consumption which made it expensive to run.

THE BEST

Ferrari is renowned for producing the world's best G.T. cars and one of the most sought after is the 250GTO. It was commonly known as 'The Ant Eater' because of its nose. Many famous names have raced in the car including Stirling Moss, Roy Salvadori and John Surtees. Only 40 cars were made between 1962 and 1964.

CHITTY, CHITTY, BANG! BANG!

This multi-purpose car could travel on land, water and in the air and was created in a book written by Ian Fleming, the author of the James Bond books. His story was based on a real car which was driven by a Polish Count at the Brooklands race track in England.

THE QUEST FOR SPEED

Donald Campbell always wanted to emulate his father, Sir Malcolm Campbell, and hold both the land and water speed records. The car he drove was called Bluebird (as were his father's cars) and was powered by a four-ton Bristol Proteus gas-turbine engine. The first attempt on the record finished in disaster with both the car and driver suffering badly. The car was rebuilt, this time with a fin at the back to keep it steady at high speeds. The next attempt was at Lake Eyre in Australia in July 1964 and, after many setbacks, Donald Campbell broke the existing record with a speed of 649 km/h (403.1 mph).

KEEPING DOWN EMISSIONS

Concern over the environment has produced legislation all over the world to cut down on emissions from motor cars. These are mostly due to incomplete combustion of the fuel and the adding of lead to stop the engine 'knocking'. Advances in engine technology and the use of catalytic converters, a sort of chemical filter, have improved the situation, as has the introduction of unleaded petrol.

STRAIGHT FROM THE SUN

This car is covered with solar panels which convert the sun's energy into the electricity needed to drive the car. On the face of it, it seems an excellent form of transport: pollution-free, no charge for fuel, easy to drive. There is always a down side. At the present stage of technology the car needs a large area to have enough solar panels to power it. The sun is important – it would be fine in Australia but not so good in Norway where there are only a few hours of sunlight per day at certain times of the year.

STEP ON THE GAS

Hyundai have produced an experimental engine powered by hydrogen gas. Cheap and easy to produce, hydrogen gas would seem to offer an excellent alternative to petrol. Pollution would be non-existent, but there would be problems with both the space required to store the gas under pressure, and the resulting lack of safety. Hybrid engines, which use either petrol or gas would seem a preferred option.

TESTING FOR SAFETY

Cars today are probably safer than they have ever been. They are tested rigorously to see how effective they are in preventing injury to driver and passengers. Here we see a simulated head-on crash in which the car is propelled forward at a set speed into a wall. It shows how front ends of cars are now built to crumple on impact and so absorb most of the shock. Side impacts are also tested, to see the efficiency of special side-impact bars built into the doors.

Cars of Today &
Cars of Tomorrow

It is always difficult to predict the future. Will the petrol engine still be with us in 50 years time? What other forms of power will be available to us? Will we even have need of personal transport? The questions are many and varied. Alternative sources of power have been with us since the dawn of motoring, but the difficulties of using them have kept them in the background. Electric cars have suffered from a shortage of range due to limited battery technology. Steam has suffered from the weight of water the car has to carry. With modern technology, this may change in the future. Gas has appeared on the scene again. There are gas filling points in some garages. Already we have instruments in the car to warn us of traffic jams ahead and to advise us on possible alternative routes. Will we be able to key our destination into the car's computer and then be whisked along by a linear motor with the technology under the road? Nothing for the driver to do except sit back and relax. Only time will tell.

BATTERY POWER

This Ford car uses electricity from a bank of batteries to power it. Very easy to drive and extremely quiet, this is an excellent car to drive. It would also seem to be pollution-free, but the electricity needed to recharge the batteries has to be produced in power stations, which are great polluters.

FASTER THAN SOUND

The first recorded land speed record was 63 km/h (39.24 mph), set by an electric car in 1898. Almost 100 years later, the record was set at 1,228 km/h (763.035 mph) by Andy Green in Thrust SSC in the Black Rock Desert, Nevada. In setting this record, he broke the sound barrier, creating a sonic boom heard 24 km (15 miles) away.

DID YOU KNOW?

The first coast-to-coast crossing of the USA was made in 1903 in a Winton car. It took 65 days, of which 20 were spent repairing the car.

The first man to drive faster than the speed of sound on land, was an American, Stan Barrett, in 1979. He drove a rocket-powered Budweiser three-wheeler, which was helped by a Sidewinder air-to-air missile. He was timed at 1,190.377 km/h (739.666 mph), but only over a distance of 16 metres (52 feet) in one direction, therefore it could not be recognized as a land speed record.

The least used world record-breaking car is the Golden Arrow. It had not been driven until it arrived in Daytona in 1929. Henry Seagrave took it on one practice run and then set a new world land speed record of 372.46 km/h (231.44 mph). It has been driven a total of about 32 km (20 miles) in all.

The Automobile Association (A.A.) was formed in 1905 to provide 'scouts' to warn motorists of police waiting in 'speed traps'. They had to stop this practice in the following year because of new laws, but managed to get round this by saying, 'If a scout doesn't salute you, ask him why. He might say that the road ahead is a little rough and you need to keep your speed down!'

The New York Police Department used steam-driven cars on patrol. They were called 'White Steamers' and followed the example of President Theodore Roosevelt, who used a similar car for his official business.

The first person to drive a motor car from Land's End to John o'Groats (from one end of Great Britain to the other) was the editor of *Autocar* magazine, Henry Sturmey. He did the trip in a 4-horsepower Coventry Daimler. The distance covered was 1,494 km (929 miles), which he covered in 93 hours, at an average speed of about 16 km/h (10 mph).

The country producing the most cars before 1906 was France, after which America took the lead. France continued to export the most cars until 1913.

At the dawn of motoring many people found starting their cars with a handle both difficult and dangerous. The introduction of the electric starter changed this situation. Although the first starter was fitted to an Arnold car in 1896, the first car with electric starting as standard was a Cadillac in 1912.

Many early cars had wooden bodies and leather mudguards. Curved boards in front of the driver's feet were a feature of early cars, to stop the dirt and stones being dashed into the car – the origin of the word 'dashboard'.

When motor car racing started, flags were used to signal the drivers. In 1899, the red flag meant 'Stop', and the yellow flag meant 'Caution'. Although there are other coloured flags in motor racing today, these two colours retain their message.

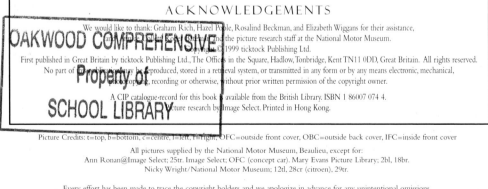

ACKNOWLEDGEMENTS

We would like to thank: Graham Rich, Hazel Poole, Rosalind Beckman, and Elizabeth Wiggans for their assistance, and the picture research staff at the National Motor Museum.

Copyright © 1999 ticktock Publishing Ltd.

First published in Great Britain by ticktock Publishing Ltd., The Offices in the Square, Hadlow, Tonbridge, Kent TN11 0DD, Great Britain. All rights reserved. No part of this publication may be reproduced, stored in a retrieval system, or transmitted in any form or by any means electronic, mechanical, photocopying, recording or otherwise, without prior written permission of the copyright owner.

A CIP catalogue record for this book is available from the British Library. ISBN 1 86007 074 4. Picture research by Image Select. Printed in Hong Kong.

Picture Credits: t=top, b=bottom, c=centre, l=left, r=right, OFC=outside front cover, OBC=outside back cover, IFC=inside front cover

All pictures supplied by the National Motor Museum, Beaulieu, except for:
Ann Ronan@Image Select; 25tr. Image Select; OFC (concept car). Mary Evans Picture Library; 2bl, 18br.
Nicky Wright/National Motor Museum; 12tl, 28cr (citroen), 29tr.

Every effort has been made to trace the copyright holders and we apologize in advance for any unintentional omissions. We would be pleased to insert the appropriate acknowledgement in any subsequent edition of this publication.